On The Edge Of Mediocrity

Kaydn Reuter

BookLeaf Publishing

Presentation by *BookLeaf Publishing*

Web: www.bookleafpub.com

E-mail: info@bookleafpub.com

ISBN: 9789357213592

First edition 2023

Self Perception

She still sleeps with a stuffed animal
And hold the pinky of every hand close
She battles life like everyone else
And strives to be an elegant war hero

She's too codependent on her imagination
And fantasizes independence
She's scared of what's in the dark
But finds peace in its tranquility

She loves the intricacy of life
Searches for purpose behind every syllable
Finds freedom in the night air
Yearns to always be the main character

She plans her future with imaginary men
Hides her emotions behind the curtain of poetry
Pretends to hate the ones she'd die without
Escapes her monsters by sleeping above them

She gets every guy but the one she wants
And criticizes every old scenario
Knows what to say days after an argument
But never in the heat of the moment

She threatens everyone harm
But will never lay a finger on you
Keeps to herself on most topics
Until you mention her hyper fixation

She takes everything seriously
But hides behind her smile
She will laugh at everything
Even when she's the only one

She's not afraid to stand up for herself
Or anyone she loves
If offended she'll belittle you eloquently
Pretend her heart is elastic

She refuses to watch anything popular
Even when she sets the standards
Has no real idea of interoception
Can barely manage her time

She forgets simple everyday tasks
But will always remember your birthday
Take every word to heart
To never apply a single consonant

She loves taking risks
Hates the consequences
Still tries to find the puzzle's missing piece
I'm glad she is me

Shining Glass

As she gazes through shining glass
Can't help but wonder and to ask
She stares at a crooked nose
Teeth light yellow when they show
Questioning all of her life choices
While all she hears are the voices

Who am I?
Who am I?

Again, she steps on a machine
Looks down as face turns green
Turned to an angle
Squeeze 'til unable
Yearning for a single gap
Gazing through shining glass

Who am I?
Who am I?

Strolling down the paved
Happiness is what's craved
See the figures
See the pictures
See something she's not

Love might fill the want
Gazing through shining glass

Who am I?
Who am I?

String lies upon her head
Watches 'til eyes go red
Hands she can't stand
Nails as thin as sand
Shredded from the ground up
Hiding that she's bound up

Who am I?
Who am I?

The outside blind it be
Inside can't find or see
Gazing through shining glass
The little girl inside
Trying hard to define

Who am I?
Who am I?

Friendship

For years I believed we would become
something more
Reminisced every moment we spent together
In my mind, you were more than just a number
to call
Even so, we didn't see eye to eye
Never seeing me as the rapunzel in your tower
Down I fell, landing in the hole I dug deeper
Surely I would be happy without a prince
Happiness of mine comes from the words yet to
form
Inside, I suppress the feelings trying so
desperately to escape
Patiently, I hold my tongue and read between the
lines

Counting Stars

It's nights like these where the sky alone takes my breath away
I look up and the cold night air fills my lungs
With a sweet satisfaction, only the stars provide
Can't help but add this to the moments I live for

When I look up for a second I forget
I forget about how excited I got to talk
Only to be returned with a single syllable
Or how when I turned for a hug
You were nowhere in sight

As I lay remembering our night all too similar
The pain of "3 days seen" sears deeper
If I count the stars like we once did
The beauty of it all temporarily washes away the pain

It's nights like this the whole world falls away
Every star glows brighter than a shine of a smile
Every grin stares back as if to say
"Here take my hand, and hold on"

As the warm embrace of the stars holds me
I stare into the infinity of it all

For merely a few seconds
Time manages to stand at a halt

1-800-662-4257

I am a dopamine addict
After the serenity prayer, I expound
Just to drive home for a fix
Counting every minute until the next high
I strive for serotonin
Work for endorphins
Beg for oxytocin
Never to any success
Spiraling into a relapse
I'm a dopamine addict

Happiness is a Butterfly

Happiness is a butterfly
Lasting merely a couple of weeks
Just to fade away
Never to be thought of again

Happiness is a butterfly
Too hard to catch
Slipping through your fingers
Just another thing to admire

Happiness is a butterfly
A symbol of what was
Fluttering through the wind
Free as can be

Drowning

For hours I watched the rain today
Cried as it gradually soaked my back
Each drop pierced my skin as if to say,
Here, remember me, let yourself crack

Little did it know, I was barely held together
The needle and thread slowly pulling apart
Dissolved by the inclement weather
Now only revealing what's left of my heart

When I snapped back to reality
Half the day had passed
As to exemplify my morality
I was unable to relax

Every morsel of water
Just a painful reminder

Late Night Thoughts

3 am thoughts never become 3 pm words
My inner dialogue never escapes
A conversation never to be heard
Every letter merely a shape

The courage of the night
Fades into wasted potential
Every urge to get right
Fails to be influential

It's simple to give up
But so hard to try
As petals of a buttercup
Away my thoughts fly

Farther my thoughts disappear
Less with my words, they cohere

Social Anxiety

I'm lonely in a crowded room
Staring into the eyes of strangers
Never quite saying the right thing
I resort to silence

Dissociating mid-conversation,
I tune into my thoughts running wild
Like a bullet train, I'm off the rails
Missing every station scheduled

Every word spoken pierces my ears
Mumbles become screams
Clapping turns to gunshots
I'd escape but the crowd is deafening

Heartbeat moves to my ears
Copper fills my mouth
I'm forced to smile through it
No one even notices

Choose to be Infinite

Don't just be the main character
Be the director of your own story
Truly living in your own reality
Making your own decisions

Choose to feel infinite
Breathlessly weightless
Read between the lines of every word
Question every syllable

Live for every moment,
Before becoming merely a memory
Let your mind smile
Allow your heart to breathe

Words mean nothing alone
Until you truly believe them
Trust means nothing without a freefall
Promises are empty if not kept

You cannot play limbo with a bar on the ground
And fly without flapping your wings
Decide to change the world
Choose to feel infinite

Memories

I don't remember much
But I forever ponder the memories
Of how you treated me as such
Now gone with the breeze

Driving from where we used to go
On the radio, our song played
remembering the world I used to know
Wondering if I should have stayed

I know I shouldn't regret
Was it just easier to run
From the memories I'll soon forget
More days are yet to come

Every memory we've made
Every memory will fade

Unrecognizable

I didn't recognize myself in the mirror today
She looked nothing like she did 5 years ago
Her hair was brushed
No sign of weariness in her eyes
Had even gained some muscle
Overall she looked healthy

For a second I forgot she was me
I peered into the eyes of what I had become
I was overwhelmingly proud
I turned those chapped lips into a grin
That same smile had won the fight

A tear fell from my face as I reminisced
Not of sorrow, but a drop of joy
I had overcome all the mountains
Endured so much pain
Now I'm proud to be unrecognizable

Existential Transportation

I've never seen a U-haul trail a hearse
No need to move into the room upstairs
It's fully furnished with bare necessities
When we say goodbye to life,
We're stripped down to our naturality
Our possessions passed down
Our names only spoken out of mouths we knew
Simply a drop in the ocean
Waiting to evaporate

Philosophical Happiness

I used to say live every day like it's prom
In my mind, prom night was perfect
A dance disguised as a fairytale
Forgetting life's troubles every step

But then I went alone
My philosophy changed
It was as magical as a penny
Hiding behind my ringing ears

Life is mediocre without someone
Wandering for a place to escape
I realized my flawed philosophy of life
And lived as my happiness depended on it

Jane Doe

To the girl who stood duller than ever
Repeating the same self deprecations
hounding her self worth like a dog
Sniffing out every flaw like prey
Yearning for affection the way one gasps for air
Instinctually needing to fill her chest once more

To the girl who was drowning in tears
her numbness rarely allowed
Wallowing in her own manure
Lathering her body with the last bit of tangible reality
Hoping to mask the emptiness left inside
Painfully aware of the stench that surrounded

To the girl who was buried alive with a plastered grin
Unaware she was becoming someone else
In her eternal search for purpose
While searching for life in a tomb,
She lied down to rest in it
Rested in the mere empty habitation of life
Burying her personality deeper with every breath

To the girl who I now long to meet
I'd like to share so many things
I wish you'd known before you left
I would begin with a hug and wipe your sweaty brow
Show you that your beauty comes from the light inside
Dim but always glowing nonetheless

To the girl who lost it all
I want to reminisce every little moment
Appreciate every story your freckles tell
Teach you that emotions are safe when guided
That it's ok to drop the plastered grin

To the girl who couldn't breathe
I wish to let you feel the independence
your lungs try to provide
I want to share every trick I've found
And show you the friends you were bound to make

To the girl whose world was crumbling down around her
I will never say that it'll be alright
Perfection is simply impossible to achieve
You'll survive, thrive even maybe
But life is still the same thing I've always lived

The same idea that existed and needed to exist
When yours was cut off so abruptly

To the girl who I shall never meet again
I would tell you to enjoy every second
Enjoy every minute passed and memory made
Because at any second it can all jolt to a stop

Paradoxical

You need to stop waiting
But patience is a virtue

You're just getting played
But that's the game of life

Spend every moment trying
But don't waste your time

Grow from your pain
But forgive and forget

Don't hate anybody
But live by the golden rule

I will never leave you
But I will follow my heart

You mean the world to me
But even that will stop spinning

You set my heart ablaze
But even bonfires dissipate

Constellations

When I gaze into the eyes as deep as stars
I get forever lost tracing those scars
Like a maze, I'm never meant to escape
Your fingers graze my neck's nape

As this story unfolds
Every page torn I hold
Gripping each piece as if it's an antique
With such delicacy and grace, I admire its physique

Never wanting the epilogue to come
I repeat every word to the desired sum
Angelically, I let every syllable flow
Likewise, I never let you go

Never tied down by gravity
Those stars become a permanent reality
Endlessly lost in the Milky Way
Forever in that gaze, I think I'll stay

Poetic Promises

Isn't it poetic how easily the switch flips
From lovers to friends we go
All depending on who we know

Isn't it poetic how I'm living merely on a promise
A promise you never dare to reciprocate
If that promise ever breaks, I would evanesce

Isn't it poetic that you ask for more time
But whenever I give mine, you disappear
Into the shadows you go, with my heart in hand

Isn't it poetic how I keep running back
Every 50-yard dash, another mile added
The finish line turning into a horizon

Isn't it poetic that I can't seem to let go
My heart is being white-knuckled by hope
The hope that this might finally unravel

Isn't it poetic how I'm in love with a puzzle piece
A piece to the wrong puzzle I try to solve
My puzzle is far from complete

Isn’t it poetic that I see the stars
Every dot in the sky counted and named for them
Every star reminds me of nights never to be replayed again

Isn’t it poetic how they’re the only thing I manage to dream about
Every thought crossing the intersection of my mind runs red
The red flags I continually neglect for the slight chance

Isn’t it poetic every mark my pen makes
Illustrated on my skin, the story of what could be
Each intrusive thought added to my skin’s dictionary

Isn’t it poetic how I used to be somebody to someone
Not just a meaningless text that flashed on a screen
Now I’m just a message to be ignored for days

Isn’t it poetic how you're still pinned on my phone
Your name hangs there like dirty laundry waiting to dry in the rain

Just always expecting for something to change

Isn't it poetic how their silence is deafening
Every word they've uttered acts as a whisper in this emphatic placidity
amidst this eerie quiet, I wait for them, just as I always said I would

Isn't it poetic that I wrote a book about them
I poured my heart out in every syllable formed
Just for those simple words, never to be returned

Please Review

All my friends think everything is worthless.
I do too, but I can't let them know this.
If I'm not the voice of reason, no one will be.
All my friends are hopelessly nihilistic.

All my friends are socially inept.
I am too, but I need to make it safe for them.
If I don't make the effort, no one will.
All my friends are anxious and depressed.

All my friends are heartbroken all the time.
I am too, but I have to pretend to be fine.
If I'm not the smiling one, no one will be.
All my friends love manipulative wastes of time.

All my friends make immature choices in life.
I do too, but I have a job and I can drive.
If I'm not the mature one, no one will be.
All my friends act so irresponsibly.

I want to be there for all of you.
Am I sufficient in doing so?
On a scale from ten to two?
I'll read every review

Under The Turtle Bridge

I'm not going to write your eulogy
Sounds harsh, I know
But you just mean too much to me

They're all just sympathy
Your life is what I'll show
So I'm not writing your eulogy

I'll bring a piece of paper empty
Since my love for you will always grow
You just mean too much to me

You can't just be a memory
Then whose clothes will I borrow
I'm not writing your eulogy

It'll break me you see
No need to visit the turtles below
You just mean too much to me

You stole my heart and lost the key
I just hope you know
I'm not going to write your eulogy
You just mean too much to me

On The Edge Of Mediocrity

I'm scraping the edge of mediocrity
Every word I write, I fall deeper
Deeper into the eyes of average
Its sum divides my heart into two

If my life was a straight line,
I'd fail my sobriety test
Left to right I lean
Under the influence of mortality

My idiosyncrasy slowly ebbs
Suffocated by simplicity
Surrounded by butterflies
I've created a chrysalis

Trapped in my own commiseration
My mosaic is too sharp to admire
Every piece stained with liquor
Exemplifying my champagne problems

I'm a caterpillar in a butterfly world
Insignificantly patternless
Thrusting out every word
Only to be drug down by the wind

I have the longevity of a wave
The tide drowns me until placid
Leaving me stranded on the beach
Dehydrated while encompassed by water

The sun burns me to the fourth degree
Peeling away all that's seared
Revealing splotches of color
Finger painted for a purpose

Art dwells underneath superficial
Words escape every cadaver
Illustrating flawed standards
Every letter doesn't sound the same

Special loses its meaning as a trend
Gifted downgrades to average
We're all just trying to survive the high tide
No matter what stroke we do

Ordinary is more than sufficient
When we escape our chrysalis
Admire our brokenness
Dance on the edge of mediocrity

www.ingramcontent.com/pod-product-compliance
Lightning Source LLC
Chambersburg PA
CBHW051758130826
49812CB00033B/1196
9789357213592